The Big Bad Wolf

Story by Dawn McMillan   Illustrations by Richard Hoit

Max and his friend Jake
met Grandpa at the school gate.

"We are in a play!" Max shouted.

"A play!" said Grandpa.

"Yes!" said Max.
"It's the *Three Little Pigs*.
I'm the big bad wolf!"

3

"And I'm the third little pig!"
said Jake.

Grandpa laughed as he helped Jake
get into the car.
"So you are going to trick the wolf!"
he said.

On Saturday, Max called out to Jake,
"Come over to my house!
Grandpa will help us with the play!"

They read the *Three Little Pigs*
over and over again.
Soon Max and Jake
could say all of the words.
Grandpa could say them, too!

"The play is on Monday," said Max.
"Please come and watch it, Grandpa."

Grandpa laughed.
"I'll be there," he said.
"I must see it."

But on Monday, when Max woke up
he didn't feel at all well.
He had a sore throat.

Grandpa looked at him.
"You have a very bad cold,"
he said.
"You will have to stay in bed."

"Oh no," cried Max.
"I can't be in the play.
Now I can't be the wolf!"

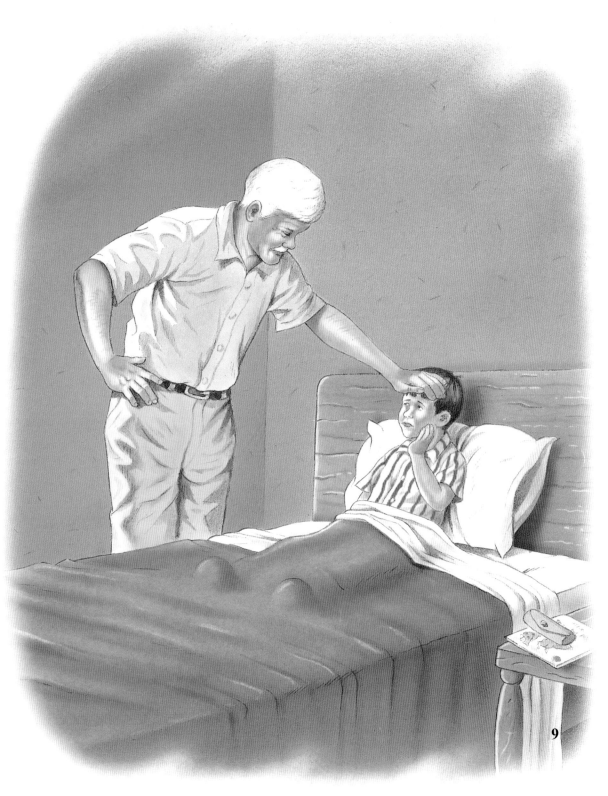

Grandpa said, "I'm sorry, Max.
But you need to stay in bed
until you are better.
I will tell your teacher."

Max felt sad.
He wanted to be in the play.
Then he looked at Grandpa.

"**You** could be the wolf," he said.
"You can say all the words.
Please, Grandpa!
Miss Green would let you."

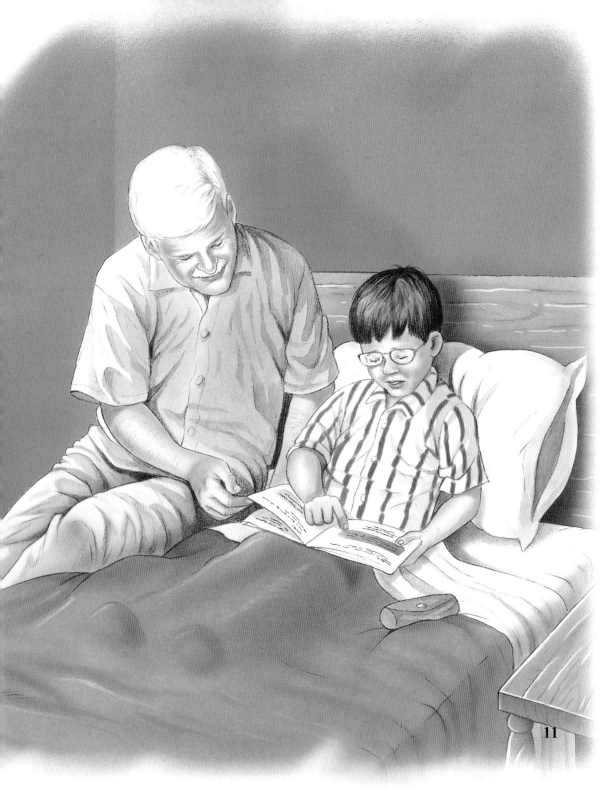

So, in the afternoon,
Jake's mom came over
to look after Max.

Grandpa went to school
to be the big bad wolf.
He had great fun.

"Little pigs, little pigs,
let me come in," said Grandpa.

"No! No!" said Jake.
"We will not let you in."

"Then I'll huff and I'll puff
and I'll **blow** your house in!"
said Grandpa.

The children loved the play.
They clapped and clapped!

Miss Green made a video.
"Max can watch our play at home,"
she said.

"And Jake's mom can watch it, too,"
said one of the children.

Max loved watching the video.
"Oh, Grandpa," he said.
"I would have been a good wolf,
but you were a **great** wolf!"